MW01118215

Coloring Bullet Journals

black bullet
JOURNAL

CPSIA information can be obtained at www.ICGtesting.com
Printed in the USA
LVOW10s0245191016

509334LV00018B/566/P

9 781537 487564